GW00570442

03908

# weblinks

You don't need a computer to use this book. But, for readers who do have access to the Internet, the book provides links to recommended websites which offer additional information and resources on the subject.

You will find weblinks boxes like this on some pages of the book.

## weblinks

For more food industry careers advice, go to www.waylinks.co.uk/series/soyouwant/food

## waylinks.co.uk

To help you find the recommended websites easily and quickly, weblinks are provided on our own website, **waylinks.co.uk.** These take you straight to the relevant websites and save you typing in the Internet address yourself.

## Internet safety

↗ Never give out personal details, which include: your name, address, school, telephone number, email address, password and mobile number.

↗ Do not respond to messages which make you feel uncomfortable – tell an adult.

↗ Do not arrange to meet in person someone you have met on the Internet.

↗ Never send your picture or anything else to an online friend without a parent's or teacher's permission.

↗ If you see anything that worries you, tell an adult.

### A note to adults

Internet use by children should be supervised. We recommend that you install filtering software which blocks unsuitable material.

## Website content

The weblinks for this book are checked and updated regularly. However, because of the nature of the Internet, the content of a website may change at any time, or a website may close down without notice. While the Publishers regret any inconvenience this may cause readers, they cannot be responsible for the content of any website other than their own.

HODDER
Wayland

So You Want to Work in the
# Food Industry?

## Margaret McAlpine

*HODDER*
*Wayland*

an imprint of Hodder Children's Books

First published in 2005 by Hodder Wayland,
an imprint of Hodder Children's Books

© Hodder Wayland 2005

Editor: Patience Coster
Inside design: Peta Morey
Cover design: Hodder Wayland

British Library Cataloguing Publication Data

McAlpine, Margaret
So you want to work in the food industry?
1. Food industry and trade - Vocational guidance - Juvenile literature
I. Title
664' . 0023

ISBN 0 7502 4581 6

Printed in China

Hodder Children's Books
A division of Hodder Headline Limited
338 Euston Road, London NW1 3BH

**Picture Acknowledgements.** The publishers would like to thank the following for
allowing their pictures to be reproduced in this publication:
Andre Perlstein/Corbis 17; Andrew Parris/APM Studios 15, 26, 27, 37, 39, 40, 41,
57, 59 (bottom); Angela Hampton Family Life Picture Library 30, 32; Charles
Gold/Corbis 42; Charles O'Rear/Corbis 38; Christopher Cormack/Corbis 14;
Chuck Savage/Corbis 44, 56; Dave Bartruff/Corbis 19 (middle); David Thomas/
PictureArts/Corbis 36; Dex Images/Corbis 52; Don Mason/Corbis 53; Eric
Robert/Corbis Sygma 12; Gregory Pace/Corbis 24; Helen King/Corbis 16, 19
(bottom); Jeff Zaruba/Corbis 55; John Henley/Corbis 54; John Madere/Corbis 47;
Jon Feingersh/Corbis 4, 9; Jose Luis Pelaez, Inc./Corbis 7, 11 (right);
Journal-Courier/The ImageWorks/Topham 33; Laureen March/Corbis 28; Leland
Bobbé/Corbis 59 (middle); Lois Ellen Frank/Corbis 11 (left), 29; Macduff
Everton/Corbis 20; Mark Peterson/Corbis 6, 8; Maximilian Stock Ltd/Science Photo
Library 48; Mediscan 34; Owen Franken/Corbis 49; Paul Barton/Corbis 25; Peter
Vadnal/Corbis 45; Pete Saloutos/Corbis 50; Philippe Caron/Corbis 13; Randy M.
Ury/Corbis 21; Reuters/Corbis 43; Robert Levin/Corbis 5; Roger Ball/Corbis 46; Roy
Morsch/Corbis 22; TEK Image/Science Photo Library 23; Tom Stewart/Corbis 31, 35;
Zul/Chapel Studios 51.

With thanks to Sam Metcalfe at Seven Dials restaurant.

**Note:** Photographs illustrating the 'day in the life of' pages are posed by models

# Contents

Words in **bold** can be found in the glossary.

# Caterer

## What is a caterer?

Caterers plan, prepare and serve food, usually for special occasions. There are times when a professional touch is required for a party or a celebration. The event may be held in a private home, but the organizers want the food to be extra special. That is when they call in the services of a caterer.

Caterers can give a business lunch or party that special touch.

Unlike chefs and cooks, caterers usually prepare food on their own premises and then take it to the place where the customer wishes it to be served. Occasionally they may prepare food in a customer's kitchen.

People use caterers for: business lunches held on company premises; dinner parties in private houses; and celebrations such as weddings, birthdays and anniversaries held in **marquees**, gardens, halls or homes.

## A special cake for a special day

At a wedding it is traditional to serve wedding cake. This can be a fruit cake, made with currants, raisins and sultanas, or a chocolate cake, or even an ice-cream cake. When the British queen, Victoria, married Prince Albert in London in 1840, their wedding cake was 3 metres (9 feet) in diameter and weighed 137 kilograms (300 pounds).

Organizations such as airlines use catering companies to provide in-flight meals. These are heated up by the airline staff during the journey.

Most caterers are self-employed, which means they work for themselves, running their own business, keeping their own accounts and finding their own catering jobs. Some caterers employ other people on a regular basis. Others take on staff for particular events to prepare food, transport it, set it out and serve it.

Caterers may be called upon for specialist assignments, such as preparing cakes for weddings.

Some customers want caterers to deliver the food and then leave the event, while others want them to stay, serve the food and clear up afterwards.

## Main tasks of a caterer

The main tasks of a caterer are to plan, cost and organize food for a particular event. Caterers meet with their customers and talk to them about the event they are planning. They discuss the date on which it is to be held and where (the venue). It is important to consider the kitchen facilities that are available. If hot food is to be served there need to be ovens; cold food needs to be stored in refrigerators.

A team of professional caterers prepares food for a customer.

The caterer and customer then discuss the type of food that is to be served. The caterer puts forward suggestions and draws up sample menus, taking into account the amount of money the customer wishes to spend and the facilities available.

## Good points and bad points

'I often receive letters from customers saying how much they enjoyed my food. It is really satisfying to feel you've helped to make a wedding or an anniversary a success.'

'Occasionally things do go wrong. The ingredients I need are not available, or staff fall ill. This is very stressful because I mustn't let customers down and spoil their special day.'

When the customer has decided on the menu, the caterer works out the costs. Once the menu and price are agreed, the caterer or the customer books the venue for the agreed date. The caterer then buys the ingredients and prepares the food for the event.

On the day, the caterer sets out the food, making it look as attractive as possible. He or she will probably stay and serve the food to the guests. Afterwards the caterer must make sure that the kitchen and the function room are left spotlessly clean.

Caterers need to make meals appear as attractive as possible and must meet food hygiene standards.

People who prepare food for sale must be registered with the **Environmental Health Service**. Caterers cooking in their own kitchens have to make sure they meet legal standards of health and **hygiene**, for example:

- food must be stored at a set temperature in a refrigerator;
- different knives and chopping boards must be used for meat and for vegetables;
- raw and cooked food must be stored separately;
- when food is being transported it must be properly packaged and kept at the right temperature.

## Skills needed to be a caterer

Caterers must be good cooks, able to produce a wide range of delicious, attractive looking food. However, other skills are just as important.

### *Financial ability*

Caterers must work out the cost of a job, taking a number of factors into account, including the price of ingredients and the time that needs to be allowed to order, prepare, transport and serve the food. They must also consider the cost of electricity, gas and petrol and the money required to pay themselves and any extra staff they need to hire. They should work out how much profit they must make, and how much of this they can put back into the business to help it grow.

Caterers are usually responsible for serving the food and drink. They must give their staff clear instructions about how to go about the work.

This profit should cover the cost of buying new equipment, such as refrigerators and ovens, replacing plates, glasses and cutlery, advertising in magazines and newspapers, and paying for the printing of brochures to promote the business.

### *Business skills*

A caterer needs a good business brain to draw up business plans and work to them, plan ahead to develop the business, deal with banks and negotiate business loans, and keep detailed accounts of his or her work.

**weblinks**

For more information on a career in catering, go to www.waylinks.co.uk/series/soyouwant/food

### Organization

Caterers need to make sure that the food preparation area is clean and orderly. They must give clear instructions to their staff, and be able to cope with the preparations for a number of events at any one time. They need to check that the correct food and the right staff are at each event.

Caterers understand that the needs of the guests are all important.

### Communication

Caterers need to be able to put customers at their ease. They must also possess the necessary sales skills to promote their business with confidence and convince people to give them work.

### Quick thinking

Many caterers work alone or with just one or two staff. When things go wrong they have to react quickly to deal with the problem.

## A day in the life of a caterer

# Jackie Sullivan

Jackie runs a catering business from her home. Before starting her business she took a three-month catering course and looked into the rules and regulations of being self-employed.

**7.30 am**     I'm off to the local market to buy fruit and vegetables.

**9.00 am**     I visit a married couple who want me to cater for the husband's retirement party. They have chosen a Chinese menu because they spent several years living in Hong Kong. Their kitchen is too small to heat food for forty guests. I suggest laying on a buffet with a Chinese theme and decorating the living-room with Chinese lanterns. The party will take place in two months' time, so I enter the date in my diary.

**11.00 am**     Back in my kitchen I start making salads for this evening. The menu is simple: cold meats and salads followed by dessert. I'm catering for one hundred people. My assistant, Sophie, arrives to help.

**1.30 pm**     Sophie and I have a cup of coffee and a sandwich while we work.

**2.30 pm**     A regular customer phones to order casseroles and pies for her freezer.

**3.00 pm**     I sort out the tablecloths, plates, glasses and cutlery for this evening.

**4.00 pm**     We load the food into the van and set off. The reception is twenty miles away. It's being held in a museum.

**6.00 pm**    Guests begin to arrive. Sophie and I serve drinks.

**6.30 pm**    I refill empty dishes with more food. Sophie is kept busy refilling guests' glasses.

**7.00 pm**    It's time to clear away the main course dishes and replace them with desserts. I check with the organizers of the event that everything is going as they wish.

**7.30 pm**    We take the trays of coffee round for the guests.

**8.30 pm**    It is almost time to start clearing away. The last guests are about to leave, but it will take us some time to pack everything away and clear up.

Caterers take telephone bookings weeks, if not months, in advance.

Only the freshest ingredients will do when buying for a special occasion.

# Chef

## What is a chef?

Chefs are people who are specially trained to plan, select and prepare foods and menus for meals served in hotels and restaurants. 'Chef' is a French word meaning 'head' or 'chief'. Many of the words used in professional cookery are French, because France has played a major part in the food and wine industries.

A chef is in charge of the food served in a restaurant, and will usually decide on the kind of menu to offer.

In schools, hospitals and canteens, the meals are less expensive than in hotels and restaurants. Here, the people doing a similar job to that of a chef are usually called cooks. They may not have as much control over the menu as chefs do, and they usually take instructions from dieticians (see page 28) and catering managers.

In fast-food restaurants and takeaways, cooks are often known as short-order cooks or quick-service cooks.

Large restaurants and hotels have kitchens divided into separate departments, each

## Monsieur Boulanger

The first eating place to be known as a restaurant was probably opened in 1765 in Paris by a Monsieur Boulanger. People had been selling food for hundreds of years, but Monsieur Boulanger was the first person to offer customers a menu with a choice of dishes.

run by a '**chef de partie**'. Each department is responsible for a particular type of work. For example, one department prepares and cooks vegetables while another makes desserts. The head chef is in charge of the whole kitchen, and he or she may well have a 'sous chef' (under chef) acting as assistant.

In a large kitchen, head chefs have a number of staff working for them.

While in training, chefs in large hotels and restaurants are known as '**commis-chefs**'. They spend time working in different departments to gain wide experience. In smaller kitchens, one chef is responsible for running the entire operation, giving instructions to everyone working in the kitchen.

## Main tasks of a chef

● Chefs plan menus making sure that there is plenty of choice for people with different tastes and special requirements. Among other things, they must consider: vegetarians who eat no meat; vegans who eat neither meat nor dairy products; Muslim and Jewish customers who do not eat pork; Hindu customers who eat no beef.

Only the freshest ingredients are used in top restaurants.

● Chefs try to ensure that their meals reflect the season, by using ingredients available at a particular time of year. Most chefs like to use fresh local produce when possible, for example, soft fruits such as strawberries and raspberries in summer.

## Good points and bad points

'Being creative and experimenting with dishes is what I enjoy. I love working with food and find the atmosphere in the kitchen exciting. At times it can be hectic, but that's part of the fun.'

'The work is physically exhausting. Although I have time off in the afternoon, it doesn't make up for working until late at night.'

- Chefs need to ensure that the cost of producing the meal is covered by the price charged for it. They must balance the price of different dishes on the menu to make sure their restaurant makes a profit. They also need to be certain that a meal can be prepared within the time allowed. Customers will want their meals served without long delays.

- Chefs must check the price, standard and availability of ingredients with their different suppliers, and understand the timescale necessary to place an order.

- Chefs are responsible for running the kitchen, making sure meals are prepared in the right way and are of a satisfactory standard.

- Chefs need to make sure that safety standards are met. They must be confident that: food preparation is carried out in a clean, hygienic environment; workers and the utensils they use are clean; washing-up and cleaning after work are carried out thoroughly; and food is stored at the right temperature.

Kitchens and food preparation surfaces must be kept spotlessly clean.

## Skills needed to be a chef

*A clear head*
The atmosphere in a restaurant kitchen can be frantic. When the restaurant is full, orders for meals arrive in the kitchen all the time. Everyone has to work very hard to keep up with them. In the best-organized kitchens things can go wrong – food is burnt, plates dropped and tempers lost. It is up to the chef to stay in control and deal with disasters of all kinds.

*Leadership skills*
Chefs have to give instructions to others and make sure they are carried out. The quality of the food served in a restaurant depends on the way chefs manage their staff.

*Love of food*
Chefs need to be excellent cooks, fascinated by food and by the different ways it can be served. Customers are always looking for new dishes to try out and it is the job of the chef to provide them with these.

*Organization*
Chefs have to plan ahead and must supervise a large number of staff, all of whom will be working on different dishes at the same time. Chefs also need to organize menus and make sure that the food offered on the menu is available and presented on time and to a high standard.

Trainee chefs learn their practical skills in the restaurant kitchen.

Food preparation has to be quick and efficient so that the customers are not kept waiting.

## fact file

Some chefs take a full-time **diploma course** in food preparation and cooking. Others take a modern **apprenticeship**, which means they learn on the job while attending college part-time.

*Communication skills*

Restaurants are where trainee chefs learn their skills. In order for them to do this, chefs need to explain clearly what they need to do and demonstrate to them how to do it. All members of staff must understand what is going on and the jobs that they have to do, so chefs need to be able to communicate their wishes very clearly and forcefully.

## A day in the life of a chef

# Suzie Rosco

Suzie is a trainee chef working in a busy restaurant. At present she is on a **work placement** from college in a small popular city centre restaurant.

**10.00 am**   I start work early because I have notes to complete. Chefs usually work a split shift covering lunchtime and evenings – so 10 am feels early to me!

**10.30 am**   The cleaners have finished in the restaurant area and work is beginning in the kitchen. A good thing about my placement is that I have a chance to try my hand at most things.

I prepare vegetables for the lunchtime trade, peeling potatoes and carrots, washing salad ingredients, topping and tailing beans. The lunchtime menu is simpler than the evening menu. Customers have less time to spend so they often order just one course and a coffee.

**11.30 am**   The chef (who is also the owner of the restaurant) gives me some tips on pastry making and I get to work on pastry cases.

**12.30 pm**   The orders start to come through from the restaurant.

**3.00 pm**   The last customers have left. The kitchen is ready for tonight. We all take our afternoon break.

**6.00 pm**   Back at work again. I make sauces for meat and fish dishes, prepare more vegetables and do whatever I'm asked to do!

| | |
|---|---|
| **6.30 pm** | Customers arrive for an early meal before going home, or to the theatre or cinema. |
| **9.00 pm** | I've been rushed off my feet for the last couple of hours. |
| **10.30 pm** | We make sure that everything is clean and in the right place. |
| **10.45 pm** | All the staff have a break while the chef talks over how the day has gone and briefs us for tomorrow. |

Chefs run kitchens in all sorts of places, as here, on a cruise ship.

Pastry making is an essential element in a chef's training.

## weblinks⟩

For more information on training and careers in the restaurant business, go to www.waylinks.co.uk/series/soyouwant/food

# Cookery Writer

## What is a cookery writer?

Cookery writers create, test and write recipes and other cooking related information for books and for magazine and newspaper articles or columns.

Cookery writing is something people tend to take up after gaining practical experience of preparing and cooking food. Cookery writers may have worked in the catering industry or run their own restaurant. Some cookery writers become well known for a certain type of cookery. They may specialize in using a particular ingredient such as fish, **game**, cheese or chocolate, or in writing about dishes from a particular part of the world, for example, China, India, Morocco, Mexico or France.

Cookery books often describe the food in faraway places as well as everyday recipes.

Today, cookery books are far more than a list of recipes. They are enjoyable to read and usually contain mouth-watering photos of different dishes. They may have personal accounts of the writers' own experiences so that readers feel they know the author. They often include

## The first lady of cookery

One of the most famous cookery writers was Mrs Beeton. She was born in 1836 and wrote the *Book of Household Management*. This book included recipes and advice on running a home and was published in instalments in a women's magazine. The book was a great success and made Mrs Beeton famous.

A good cookery book is a vital ingredient for the home kitchen.

photos of the landscape of a particular area featured in the cookery book, and descriptions of local customs. Cookery books may also be written to accompany a cookery series on television.

Cookery writers in magazines and newspapers are often trained journalists who have developed an interest in food and started writing about it. They may be food critics, whose job is to eat out at restaurants and then write about the quality of the meals and the service they received.

**weblinks**

For more information on careers in cookery writing and journalism, go to www.waylinks.co.uk/series/soyouwant/food

## Main tasks of a cookery writer

Famous cooks may be approached by a publisher and asked to write a book. Those who are less well known may contact publishers with their ideas and try to find one who is interested in hiring them. Magazine and newspaper writers usually have a contract to write a monthly or weekly column for a set fee and for a fixed period of time.

A new recipe might sound good, but what will it taste like?

- Cookery writers are always looking for new recipes or ways of preparing food. This can involve research, for example, by: reading existing cookery books for new ideas; visiting restaurants; and travelling to different countries to find out what people eat and how they prepare their food.

## Good points and bad points

'I love writing and I love cooking, so I'm very lucky to have a job that involves both. I often plan my holidays around ideas for books so I can wander round local food shops and eat in restaurants.'

'A lot of time is spent on routine checking, making sure that everything I've written is correct. If a recipe doesn't work, readers are very quick to complain. Proof-reading takes quite an effort because by this stage I'm ready to move on to something new.'

- The next step for a cookery writer is to test out recipes and adapt them where necessary. This could involve: replacing ingredients that are expensive or difficult to find; simplifying the preparation and cooking to appeal to modern cooks who lead busy lives; and adjusting the quantity of the ingredients so that the dish will feed a set number of people (usually four or six).

- The cookery writer must then put together the recipes and other material in an interesting logical order.

- The cookery writer works closely with designers and food photographers to make sure that the different elements of the book (the visuals) are presented in a clear and attractive way.

- The writer needs to check the book or magazine as it will look when it is printed, for any final mistakes.

After the research and planning are complete, there is the writing to do.

- The writer helps to attract publicity, which will help sell the book, by: signing copies of the book in bookshops and giving talks to different groups of people; and appearing on television and speaking on the radio.

## Skills needed to be a cookery writer

Cookery books are a favourite choice for birthday and Christmas gifts and are read by people for pleasure as well as information. Writers obviously need to have a real interest in and fascination for food, because they spend most of their working lives thinking about it, talking about it and writing about it. However, other skills are equally important if a writer is to produce a successful cookery book.

If you are a famous personality, like the Duchess of York, it certainly helps in selling your cookery book!

*Research*

Readers are always looking for something new, and cookery writers spend a lot of time thinking up new ideas for books and articles and recipes to go in them. Famous cookery writers have researchers carrying out this work for them, but those who are less well known do their own research.

*Cookery skills*

Writers must be able to prepare and cook dishes successfully before they can give instructions to other people on how to cook.

*Writing skills*

Writers need to have a clear, lively style of writing. Cookery books and articles should be interesting to read, with straightforward instructions that are easy to follow.

A book needs to be well designed and have attractive illustrations if it is to sell well.

*Communication skills*
Writers have to talk about their books and even demonstrate their recipes in public and on television.

## fact file

Some people simply have a good idea for a book and are lucky enough to find a publisher. Other cookery writers are either professionally trained in catering or in journalism.

*Teamwork*
Cookery writers do not work alone. They are part of a team, including **editors**, photographers, designers and publicity professionals. All these people are involved in the process, and they must all communicate clearly with one another if they are to succeed in producing a good cookery book.

## A day in the life of a cookery writer

## Shara Madi

Shara grew up in Turkey and learnt to cook from her mother. She has written several cookery books on Eastern European food.

**7.30 am**  I'm at work early because I need to have the first version of my new book ready to send to my publisher today. I work from an office at my home.

**9.00 am**  I'm feeling pleased with myself because I've done a lot of work. The phone hasn't rung once so I've been able to get on with it. I make myself a cup of coffee and take my daughter to school.

**11.00 am**  I spoke too soon! I've been on the phone to my editor for the past hour. He wants to arrange a meeting with the designer and me to discuss how the book is to look. He also wants to see any photos my family has of life in Turkey. He has a lot of interesting ideas, but I need to get on!

**12.00 pm**  I receive a phone call from a television company that would like to use some of my recipes in a cookery programme. That could be exciting.

Detailed research is an important first step to writing a good book.

There are lots of interesting cookery books on sale in shops today.

**12.30 pm**　My daughter's school rings to say she is ill and needs to be collected. I stop work and go to fetch her.

**2.00 pm**　My daughter has a sore throat. I try to do some work while she sleeps. I find a note saying that I need to check the ingredients for one of my recipes in the book. This is a blow because I thought I'd already done it.

**4.30 pm**　I make my daughter a warm drink and do some more work while she watches a cartoon.

**7.00 pm**　My partner returns home from work, and the family are together now. We've had supper, so I go back to work for another hour or so.

# Dietician

Dieticians understand scientifically how the human body reacts to food. They use this information to educate people about healthy eating and to encourage them to eat properly.

In recent years there has been a lot of publicity on television and in newspapers about the harmful effects of bad eating habits on people of all ages. Poor diet can mean either eating too much of the wrong types of food, such as crisps and sweets, or not eating enough of the right types of food, for example, fruit and vegetables.

Healthy eating is an important part of keeping fit.

## Burger king

In 1895, the first hamburgers were served at Louis' Lunch sandwich shop in New Haven, Connecticut, in the USA. Louis Lassen ran a stall selling steak sandwiches to local workers. After trimming the meat to fit the bread, he would mince the leftovers, grill them, put them between two slices of bread and sell them.

A good diet is very important. If adults eat the wrong kinds of food they can become overweight and therefore unable to lead active, interesting lives. They may also develop heart problems and other conditions, such as **diabetes**. Children who eat unhealthy diets can become very overweight, or they may fail to grow properly because their diets lack vital **nutrients**.

Eating too much of the wrong type of food can cause health problems.

The work of a dietician includes:

- helping people who already have a problem, discussing the changes they could make to their diet;
- making sure that people understand the need to eat healthily, talking to different groups such as teenagers, young parents and older people about the food they need to eat in order to keep fit and well;
- drawing up special diets for individuals with particular problems, such as diabetes.

**weblinks**

For more information on training and a career as a dietician, go to www.waylinks.co.uk/series/soyouwant/food

## Main tasks of a dietician

Dieticians carry out their work in different surroundings and in different ways. Many work in hospitals, with patients who need to adapt their diets to cope with an illness or condition. For example: patients with diabetes need help to control their blood sugar levels; patients with heart problems need advice on reducing their intake of rich fatty foods and increasing their intake of vegetables; and parents of children with **allergies** to, for example, dairy or wheat products, need to be told about alternative foods.

Some patients who are not physically ill may need help to deal with eating disorders, such as: anorexia – patients suffering from this condition believe they are fat and refuse to eat normally; and bulimia – patients are convinced they are overweight, so they make themselves sick after meals to stop putting on weight.

Helping children to learn the difference between healthy and unhealthy foods is very important.

## Good points and bad points

'As more is becoming known about the effect that types of food have on the human body, so my job becomes more interesting.'

'I enjoy my work, but I do find it depressing to see the amount of junk food eaten by children.'

Dieticians need to offer patients such as these a great deal of support to encourage them to eat healthily.

Dieticians advise hospital catering staff on how to prepare healthy, balanced meals. Different dietary requirements may include those of patients and staff who are vegetarians or vegans or whose religion means they need specially prepared foods.

In a similar way, dieticians also work with patients in the community, for example in schools, health centres and **parenting classes**. They talk to groups in the community and give advice on healthy eating.

Dieticians work for food production companies, advising on new products, writing the **nutritional** information that is included with products and checking that it is correct. There are job opportunities for dieticians in all sorts of organizations. They may find themselves suggesting and creating healthy menus in many different settings, including schools, colleges and airlines.

## Skills needed to be a dietician

*Scientific knowledge*
A dietician needs to have a knowledge and understanding of science so that he or she can analyze diets and develop new ones to meet particular needs.

*Communication skills*
Dieticians must be able to communicate clearly with their patients, many of whom are children. They need to explain the effects that the food people eat can have on their bodies. This involves explaining complicated medical and scientific matters in a simple way, using everyday words that are easily understood. Some dieticians give talks to groups of people in the community. To do this well they need to be able to speak in an interesting, lively way.

*Tact*
People usually find it very difficult to change their eating habits. Dieticians need to help patients move forward without making them feel that they are to blame for their situation. People with eating problems are often depressed and lonely and can be easily upset. They feel guilty about having a problem and need to be helped to feel better about themselves.

Dieticians need to encourage patients to make changes to their diet.

*Patience*
Changes do not happen overnight. Patients can easily return to their old bad habits for a while and it can take a long time for progress to be made.

Here a dietician answers questions during a tour of a grocery store.

Dieticians need to remain positive and encouraging towards patients who may be finding it difficult to help themselves.

*Teamwork*
Dieticians work closely with other people, including nurses, doctors, the patients themselves and their families.

*Interest in new developments*
Research is revealing more and more about how the human body reacts to food. Dieticians need to keep up-to-date with the latest developments.

## fact file

Dieticians must complete a first or second degree in **dietetics** or human nutrition and dietetics, followed by registration with the **Health Professions Council**.

## A day in the life of a dietician

## George Davis

George is a dietician working in a hospital. He graduated from university with a degree in dietetics and has been working for fourteen years.

**8.45 am**   I check my diary and emails.

**9.30 am**   A meeting with the **paediatric** medical team to discuss children with food allergies on the ward.

**10.30 am**   I meet with the catering manager to talk over menus. This is a difficult job. Meals have to meet certain nutritional standards. There have to be alternatives for people with special dietary and religious needs. Food has to be healthy and look attractive and all this needs to be done on a very tight budget.

**12.00 pm**   Administration time for phone calls, letters and emails.

**1.45 pm**   I feel quite hungry and have a sandwich in the canteen.

**2.30 pm**   I attend the outpatients clinic. My first appointment is with parents of an overweight six-year-old. We talk about ways of improving the family diet and make an appointment for a month's time to see how things are going.

Dieticians need to be on the look out for problems before they lead to serious illness.

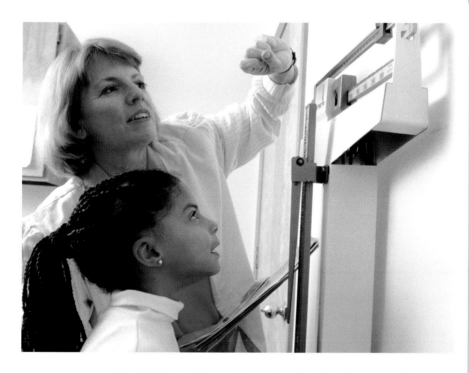

The dietician advises patients what they should eat to avoid ill-health. The dietician may often check for weight gain or loss.

**3.30 pm**  I see a very slim mother with an underweight toddler. This mother is very weight conscious and visits the gym regularly. She says her daughter doesn't have a big appetite. I draw up some menu suggestions and ask the mother to try them and come back in a couple of weeks.

**4.30 pm**  I phone the child's doctor. The toddler is not thriving and I am concerned about what she is being given to eat.

**5.00 pm**  I meet a colleague in the corridor who asks me if I would give a talk to a group of people recovering from heart attacks. I agree to do it, and look for a free space in my diary!

# Food Photographer

## What is a food photographer?

Food photographers take pictures of different types of food for use in cookery books, magazines, newspapers and advertisements. Most food photographers are **freelance**. They usually start their careers as photographic assistants working with established photographers.

Food photography takes a lot of planning and the photographs have to be taken quickly because food does not look good for very long. This means that getting the right food shot is not easy. Most food photography takes place in a studio rather than on location. The dishes to be photographed are prepared and cooked by **food stylists**. These are specialist cookery professionals who know how to prepare food and make it look good in front of the camera.

Food photographers should make readers feel hungry!

The work of food photographers has changed with the arrival of **digital photography**. The **shooting process** has been made easier, because there is no actual film involved so there is no need to reload the camera. However, a great deal of work now takes place after the photos have been taken.

## Food models

It is not always possible to find the right food for a photographic **shoot**. Food such as fresh fruit may be out of season, or too fragile to photograph well. One choice open to designers or photographers is to use models of food. These are made by professional modellers and are expensive because a lot of work is involved in making them. However, sometimes the cost is worthwhile if it ensures a selection of good photographs.

The photographer meets with the client before the shoot to discuss exactly what kinds of photographic effects are required.

Advanced computer programmes mean that once the images have been loaded on to a computer they can be combined in many different ways. For example, food shots taken in a studio can be combined with a photo of a picnic on a mountainside, so that the food looks as though it is really part of the picnic. Special effects, such as splash shots, can capture the moment an object – for example, an ice-cube – hits water in a tumbler and causes a splash.

In the past, if a photo was not absolutely right, a re-shoot would be needed. Now photos can be **retouched** on a computer to remove imperfections such as a smear of sauce on a plate or a wilting lettuce leaf.

## Main tasks of a food photographer

The key to a successful photo shoot is planning. The designer, food photographer and food stylist work together at this stage. They decide: what shots are needed; how the shots are to look (composition); what props (extra items such as glasses, fruit and flowers) will be used, and the type of lighting required.

The team makes technical decisions, for example, whether to use food models instead of real food. The lighting, food and background may take several hours to prepare. At the last minute, final touches need to be made. These include coating supposedly hot food with oil to make it look as though it has just come out of the oven. Other tricks of the trade include adding fresh herbs at the last possible moment so they do not have time to wilt, and positioning food such

There is a lot to learn in the technical side of photography.

## Good points and bad points

'No two days are the same and I meet lots of different people.'

'Food photography is often seen as the poor, unglamorous relation of fashion photography.'

The photographer's assistant arranges props in readiness for the shoot.

as chocolate, which melts very quickly; also, an icing sugar mixture is often used as a substitute for ice cream, which loses its shape in seconds.

The taking of the photos is known as the shoot. Food photographers usually work with an assistant, who does all the odd jobs such as looking after cameras and moving props. After the shoot there is post-production, which involves preparing the photos for the designer. As the use of digital photography increases, photographers are able to carry out more and more adjustments on screen.

## weblinks▸

For more information about working as a food photographer, go to www.waylinks.co.uk/series/soyouwant/food

## Skills needed to be a food photographer

*Artistic ability*

A food photographer needs to have good creative ideas about the ways in which food can be made to look tempting.

*Technical skills*

Food photographers must know how to achieve different effects with lighting. They need to be able to use cameras and different types of photographic equipment with confidence. The book designer and food stylist both rely on the photographer for technical advice.

*Computer skills*

Digital photography is replacing traditional photography in many fields, including food photography. It is uncertain whether there will always be a place for traditional cameras using film, or whether these will be replaced entirely by digital cameras. What is certain is that digital cameras give photographers great opportunities to use specialist computer programmes to:

The food photographer adds the final touches to a dish before photographing it.

- touch-up photos;
- change backgrounds;
- combine two or more pictures;
- remove unwanted items such as crumbs or smears of food.

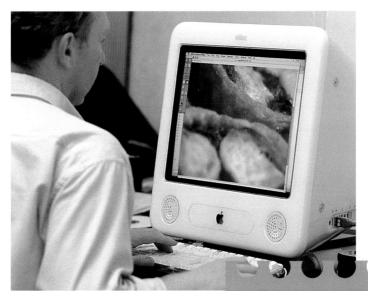

Digital photography means that computers are used to alter, and often dramatically improve, images.

## fact file

Most photographers have a degree or diploma in photography. However impressive their qualifications, the way to becoming a food photographer is through finding freelance work as a photographer's assistant.

*Patience*

Hours of planning are involved in a successful shoot. Food photographers need to spend time talking to clients about what they want and then put a lot of effort into achieving this.

*Teamwork*

Food photographers need to enjoy working closely as part of a team with designers and food stylists.

*Determination*

Professional photography is often seen as a glamorous job. There is fierce competition for work and finding it is tough. Photographers need to be able to sell themselves and their work and cope with rejection and disappointment.

## A day in the life of a food photographer

# Lee Hacker

Lee took a professional photography course. He then did some work as a fashion photographer, before specializing in food photography.

**8.30 am**   I spend some time doing my accounts, sending out invoices and chasing up money I am owed. As I am self-employed, I have to allow time for paperwork.

**10.00 am**   I phone a couple of people who might be able to give me some work in the future. Making and keeping up with contacts is important.

**10.30 am**   I have a meeting with a well-known food and drink photographer. I began my career working as his assistant. I've learned a great deal from him and he is very well respected in the industry. He wants me to work with him on a couple of projects in the future.

**12.00 pm**   I get in the car and make the hour long drive to see the marketing manager of a food production company.

If the photographer does a good job, the food looks so delicious, it's hard to resist.

She is going to **commission** a photographer to take some advertising shots. We talk over what she is looking for. I show her my **portfolio** and hope she's impressed.

**4.30 pm**  Back home I check my emails and listen to my answerphone. There's a message from a contact asking me to meet him this evening. I have to get up at 6.00 am tomorrow for a shoot which is likely to last about twelve hours, so I'm desperate for an early night. However, my contact tells me there could be a job coming up and I can't afford to miss the chance of work, so I agree to meet him.

**5.00 pm**  The marketing manager I met earlier phones to say I've got the job. We discuss the fee and she asks me to prepare for the shoot, starting in two weeks' time.

Digital cameras enable food photographers to shoot as many images as they like, without having to reload the film.

# Food Technologist

## What is a food technologist?

Food technologists study the scientific nature of food
and the way it reacts under certain conditions. They
work for food preparation and **processing** companies
and research organizations, making sure what we eat
tastes good and is of a high quality.

The choice of
convenience
foods available
today is
enormous.

In the last half century much has changed in the field
of food preparation. Fifty years ago, most married
women did not work. They
shopped for fresh meat and
vegetables several times a
week and cooked meals for
their families every day.
Once a week, they would
bake cakes, pies and biscuits.

Today, most women have
jobs outside the home and
spend less time than their
grandmothers did buying
food and preparing meals.
People's tastes have also
changed. Families now enjoy
recipes from around the
world and would find the
meals of fifty years ago
quite boring.

## Empire of ice

Believe it or not, the creator of the modern frozen food industry was Clarence Birdseye! He lived in Canada in around 1912 and trapped animals for food. Birdseye noticed that food frozen in midwinter tasted better than food frozen at warmer times. He realized that the faster the freezing process, the less chance there was of ice crystals damaging the food. He made a fortune by using this fast-freeze knowledge to set up a business empire.

A great many people are employed in food production and processing.

People today buy a great deal of prepared or **convenience meals**. The average family refrigerator and freezer usually contain an assortment of foods that need only to be defrosted and heated before they can be eaten.

At the same time, outbreaks of food poisoning and fears about the quality of the food being eaten have made the public conscious of the need for high standards in food production and preparation. This has led to an increased demand for food technologists.

## Main tasks of a food technologist

Food technologists work on developing new food products and improving existing ones. Their job includes research into different aspects of food production, such as lengthening shelf life, in other words, keeping food fresh and fit to eat for longer periods of time.

Research work also involves simplifying cooking and serving methods. When time is short, shoppers want meals that are already cooked and only need reheating. The easier it is to heat these meals and put them on the table, the more popular they will be. Food technologists also research how to improve the flavour of food. Whether the food is ready prepared, canned, or frozen, people still want their meals to taste as if they were freshly cooked that day.

Food technologists test out new recipes before they go on sale.

## Good points and bad points

'There's not much I don't like about my job. I enjoy working in a laboratory and the work I do is interesting and varied.'

'It's not usually a problem, but I do need to concentrate on what I am doing all the time, because the slightest slip, such as making a mistake reading the result of an experiment, could cause major difficulties for my company.'

Food technologists have to look ahead, because tastes are always changing. One year, Thai food is popular and the next year, Italian. Before a new recipe is sold to the public, technologists run trials on small batches of food to sort out any problems.

Food technologists check that food produced in a factory meets set standards for size, colour and taste. Consumers expect all the biscuits in a packet to be the same size and colour, with the same amount of jam or icing.

There are strict regulations about the way food is produced, stored and sent out to shops and restaurants. It is the job of food technologists to set up systems to make sure these regulations are met. Failure to do this can result in **epidemics** of food poisoning, which cause serious illness.

Checking that food production conditions are of a high standard is part of a food technologist's job.

## Skills needed to be a food technologist

*Scientific abilities*

Food technologists need to have a high level of knowledge in subjects such as biology, physics and chemistry to understand the scientific reasons for changes in food. They also need to be competent at mathematics to deal with numerical calculations.

*Problem-solving*

Food technologists need to be able to think around a problem in order to find a solution.

*Teamwork*

The work of food technologists involves close contact with large numbers of people including:

- other members of the food technology team;
- the food development team, who work on new recipes;
- dieticians, who are concerned with the nutritional quality of the food;
- **economists**, who work out the cost of producing food and suggest the price at which it should be sold;
- **food production operatives**, who produce the food in large quantities for sale.

Food technologists need to be interested in food from a scientific point of view. These technologists are sampling cheese.

### An eye for detail

Food technologists need to be able to focus on a project and study it in great detail. It is important that they notice the smallest changes that occur.

This food technologist is testing cacao for use in chocolate production.

### Patience

Food trial projects can take a long time to complete, so food technologists need to be patient as they wait for the results.

### Flexibility

Food technologists often work on more than one project at a time, so they must be flexible enough to move swiftly from one to another with ease.

### Communication skills

The food technologist's job involves explaining his or her findings to other people, including those who do not have a high level of scientific knowledge.

### Computer skills

Today, food technologists use computers frequently for many reasons, including doing research, storing information and producing reports.

## fact file

Food technologists need a degree or a diploma in a subject such as food technology, food science, or food studies. Some have a degree in another science subject, followed by a further degree in food technology.

## A day in the life of a food technologist

# Harry Chung

Harry is a trainee food technician at a research company that solves problems for large food preparation and manufacturing companies. Harry's company offers training courses that are attended by food technologists from all parts of the world.

**9.00 am**     I am settled in the lab where I spend most of my working day. The company works on a flexi-time scheme and I often come in early to get on with my work. Today is quite a late start for me.

**9.30 am**     At present I'm involved in several projects. This morning I'm testing different food ingredients to find out their nutritional values. It is important that these values are correct so the right information is given on the product packaging.

**11.30 am**     I meet with my manager to talk over the progress I'm making and to look at my findings. As a research company, we have an international reputation, of which we're very proud.

**1.30 pm**     Time for a break. Working with food doesn't put me off my lunch and as soon as I reach the canteen I realize how hungry I am!

The results of tests are stored on computer.

**2.15 pm**    I check the data and start working on a report. I've been involved in a project checking the instructions that manufacturers provide for customers when they buy convenience food. Now I have to write up my findings.

**5.30 pm**    The report took me longer to write than I'd planned, so I shall need to make an early start tomorrow.

**7.30 pm**    My ambition is to specialize in dietary advice for sports people. I am preparing a talk that I am to give at a golf club, so I spend a couple of hours working on that.

In today's busy world, families take advantage of convenience foods like TV dinners that are quick and easy to prepare.

## weblinks

For more information about a career in food science and technology, go to
www.waylinks.co.uk/series/
soyouwant/food

# Restaurant Manager

Restaurant managers are the link between the staff in the restaurant kitchen preparing the food, the staff who serve customers at the tables, and the customers themselves.

Restaurant managers are in charge of the restaurant and make sure that: the food is good; the customers are happy; the staff are doing their jobs properly; and the business is making money.

A restaurant needs to look inviting to attract customers.

## The birth of McDonald's

Richard and Maurice McDonald founded McDonald's Restaurant in 1948 in San Bernadino, California. The first 'Big Mac' hamburger was sold in 1968 and the first 'drive-thru' McDonald's was opened in 1975. Today there are more than 30,000 McDonald's restaurants in well over one hundred countries.

Some restaurants belong to a group or chain, which owns dozens, hundreds or even thousands of outlets. All these restaurants are decorated in the same way and look very similar to one another. They offer the same menus at the same time. At the group headquarters, senior staff make decisions for these restaurants and send out instructions to the different branches. It is the job of the restaurant managers to see that these instructions are carried out.

Making people feel welcome is the first step to ensuring that they enjoy themselves.

Independent restaurants are not part of a chain. They attract customers by developing their own style of décor and food. In these restaurants, the manager is responsible for planning business activities, making decisions and putting these into practice. In some cases, managers are also the owners of their restaurants.

## Main tasks of a restaurant manager

Restaurant managers are responsible for different areas of activity in the restaurant.

Restaurant managers' work is front-of-house – which means that they deal with the public, meeting customers and making them feel at home. They make sure that:

- the restaurant is clean and tidy and looks inviting;
- customers are greeted as soon as they arrive, and are found a table;
- customers are given menus, and orders for food and drink are taken promptly;
- complaints are dealt with politely and promptly.

They supervise staff at the restaurant by:

- interviewing and recruiting;
- organizing training sessions;

Restaurant managers must ensure that their staff are properly trained, suitably dressed and polite.

# Good points and bad points

'I enjoy meeting people, and seeing them having a good time gives me a lot of satisfaction.'

'The hours are long. I work most evenings and at weekends, so I don't have much opportunity to enjoy a social life outside the restaurant.'

- drawing up work and holiday **rotas** to make sure there are always enough staff on duty;
- dealing with any discipline problems and dismissing staff when necessary.

Restaurant managers control the money spent in the restaurant. Together with the chef, they set the prices of meals. They are also responsible for looking after the money taken in the restaurant. This involves:

- checking the money taken and making sure it **tallies** with the receipts for meals;
- entering these figures into the **book-keeping** system;
- making sure the money is delivered safely to the bank.

In restaurants that are not part of a chain, managers need to think of ways to develop business. These may involve:

- organizing special menus, for example, Chinese nights, Indian nights, wine-tastings, party nights;
- thinking of ideas for special offers, such as discounts for parties, and meal vouchers in magazines and newspapers;
- placing advertisements in the local press.

Restaurant managers also organize the redecoration of the restaurant and the replacement of furniture, crockery and cutlery.

Staff need to work together as a team, and part of the restaurant manager's job is to make sure that they do.

## Skills needed to be a restaurant manager

*Communication and leadership skills*
Restaurant managers spend most of their time dealing with customers, suppliers and members of staff, so they need to get on well with different types of people. They have to be fair but firm, and need to motivate staff to work hard. They should do their best to make sure customers relax and enjoy themselves.

*Stamina*
Restaurant managers work long hours, so they need plenty of energy and staying power. They may have a break when the restaurant is closed during the late afternoon, but they must be prepared to deal with paperwork or planning during this time. They spend a lot of time on their feet and may have to take on any job when necessary.

Managers are in charge of the restaurant budget, which includes ordering and paying for goods.

*Business skills*
Restaurant managers need to understand how a business works and must be competent in finance, administration and sales and marketing.

*Enthusiasm*
Managers need to be cheerful and positive about their work at all times, even when it is past midnight and customers are still in the restaurant.

**weblinks**
For more information about training and careers in the restaurant business, go to www.waylinks.co.uk/series/soyouwant/food

Emptying the till at the end of the day is another task for the restaurant manager.

## fact file

Restaurant managers need several years experience working in the catering and food industry. Some restaurant managers have a degree or a diploma in a subject such as hotel and catering management. Others have gained practical experience through working as waiters, kitchen assistants or chefs.

*Quick thinking*

Whether it is electricity failure, a double booking or an angry customer – the manager has to sort out the problem swiftly, while trying to make sure other customers are not embarrassed or upset.

Difficult situations can arise, even in the best-run restaurants. Most customers are polite and just want to enjoy themselves, but occasionally a person can be rude or difficult. When this happens, the manager needs to keep his or her temper and deal quietly but firmly with the situation. Restaurant managers who keep their tempers help customers to keep theirs.

## A day in the life of a restaurant manager

## Jane Stokes

Jane owns and manages a restaurant she set up with a chef, who is also her best friend. The restaurant has been running for four years and its atmosphere is relaxed and informal. It is a small operation, with two kitchen assistants and two waiters, but Jane is hoping to expand it in future.

| | |
|---|---|
| **9.30 am** | I check that the restaurant is clean and tidy and make sure that tablecloths and napkins are back from the laundry. Jack the chef and I discuss changes to the menu. He's keen to introduce more fish dishes. |
| **10.00 am** | Staff arrive and set the tables. I go into my office to pay bills and organize some publicity. |
| **12.30 pm** | The restaurant is getting busy, so I come out and take some orders. |
| **3.00 pm** | The staff leave for the afternoon. Jack and I have a meeting with an architect about enlarging the restaurant. A kitchen assistant rings to say she can't work tonight. I eventually find a replacement. |
| **4.00 pm** | I go home for a shower and a sandwich. |
| **5.00 pm** | I'm back at the restaurant. Staff arrive for the evening shift. |
| **6.00 pm** | Business is quiet, so I check last month's figures. |

**7.30 pm**   A young man arrives with his girlfriend and insists that he reserved a window table. I look in the reservations book and see nothing about the window. My customer is angry and starting to raise his voice. I apologize for the situation and give him a free bottle of wine. I've learned through experience that unpleasant scenes give diners indigestion, which isn't good for business!

**8.00 pm**   A busy evening – I'm taking orders non-stop.

**11.30 pm**   Time to go home.

If customers are enjoying themselves, then the restaurant manager's job can be said to have been well done.

At smaller restaurants, the manager's job can range from hiring staff to waiting on tables herself.

# Glossary

allergies – sensitive reactions of the body, such as sore skin or rashes.

apprenticeship – a training period during which a young person learns how to do a job.

book-keeping – keeping a documented record of money spent and money earned.

chef de partie – the person in charge of a department in a restaurant kitchen.

commis-chef – a trainee working in a restaurant kitchen, learning how to cook.

commission – a request to do a particular piece of work.

convenience meals – ready-made meals, usually shop bought, that are quick and easy to prepare.

décor – the design and decoration of a room.

diabetes – an illness affecting sugar levels in the human body.

dietetics – the study of healthy eating.

digital photography – pictures taken using a computerized camera. Digital photos can be transferred directly on to a computer screen.

diploma course – study at college leading to a qualification which is just below degree standard.

economist – a person who studies ways in which money is spent.

editor – a person in charge of producing a book, magazine or newspaper.

Environmental Health Service – an organization that makes sure food is made, stored and sold in clean conditions.

epidemic – outbreak of an illness or disease affecting a large number of people.

food production operative – a person preparing food on a production line in a factory.

food stylist – a person who prepares food for photography shoots, cooking and arranging it so that it looks attractive and appetizing.

**freelance** – not employed by any particular organization or person; a person who works for him or herself and carries out jobs for a range of different people.

**game** – animals and birds that are traditionally hunted for food, for example, deer, rabbits, pheasant and grouse.

**Health Professions Council** – an organization that oversees the standard of training and qualifications needed to work in different jobs in the health sector.

**home economics teacher** – a person giving lessons in school on the basics of healthy eating and the preparation of nutritious meals.

**hygiene** – standards of cleanliness needed to keep people healthy.

**marquee** – a very large tent used for celebrations.

**nutrients** – nourishing substances found in food.

**nutritional** – to do with food.

**paediatric** – to do with children's health. A paediatric nurse cares for sick children.

**parenting classes** – training for mothers and fathers to help them care for children in the right way.

**portfolio** – a large case for carrying papers. Photographers put together portfolios of their work to show their skills to people.

**processing** – preparing or working on something.

**retouched** – removing faults such as crumbs in a photograph. Retouching is often carried out using computer techniques.

**rota** – a list of people giving the dates and times they are to do something, usually work.

**shoot** – a session during which photographs are taken.

**shooting process** – the period spent preparing for and taking photographs.

**tallies** – agrees with.

**work placement** – time spent by students or young people in a work situation so they can see what the job is really like.

# Further Information

## So do you still want to work in the food industry?

This book does not aim to cover every job in the food and catering industries, and many, including those of food stylist and **home economics teacher**, are missing.

What it does hope to do is to give you an idea of the range of different jobs, and what working in them is really like. There are many interesting careers in the food and catering industries, not just working in restaurants, but in hospitals, schools and laboratories. There are careers in which you can train to advise people on healthy eating. In contrast, there are also opportunities to work in food photography and journalism.

The way to find out if a job in the food industry is right for you is to discover as much as you can about the work. Try reading books on the subject and talking to people who have jobs in that area.

If you are at secondary school and seriously interested in a certain career, ask your careers teacher if he or she could arrange for some work experience. This means spending some time, usually a week or two, in an area of your chosen profession. In this instance, you could go to a hotel, a restaurant, a laboratory or another working environment which interests you.

## Books

If you want to find out more about working in the food and catering industries, you will find the following helpful:

*Guide to Careers in Hospitality, Tourism and Leisure*, written by Caroline Ritchie, published by Hobsons, 2001.

*Guide to Working in the Hospitality Industry*, written by Caroline Ritchie, Russell Joseph, published by Kogan Page, 1998.

*Working in Hotels and Catering*, written by Beryl Dixon, Careers and Occupational Information Centre, 1999.

*Working in Photography*, Careers and Occupational Information Centre, 1998.

*Working in Publishing and Journalism*, written by Paul Kingston, Careers and Occupational Information Centre, 2001.

### weblinks

For more food industry careers advice, go to
**www.waylinks.co.uk/ series/soyouwant/food**

# Useful addresses

## United Kingdom

### Cookery Writer
National Council for the
Training of Journalists
Latton Bush Centre
Southern Way
Harlow
Essex
CM18 7BL
Tel: 01279 430009

### Dietician
The British Dietetic
Association
Fifth Floor
Charles House
148-149 Great Charles
Street
Birmingham
B3 3HT
Tel: 0121 200 8080

NHS Careers
PO Box 376
Bristol
BS99 3EY
Tel: 0845 60 60 655

### Food Technologist
Institute of Food Science
and Technology
5 Cambridge Court
210 Shepherds Bush Road
London
W6 7NJ
Tel: 020 7603 6316

### Chef/Restaurant Manager
Academy of Culinary Arts
53 Cavendish Road
London
SW12 0BL
Tel: 020 8673 63000

British Institute of
Innkeeping
Wessex House
80 Park Street
Camberley
Surrey
GU15 3PT
Tel: 01276 684449

British Hospitality and
Restaurant Association
Queen's House
55-56 Lincoln's Inn Fields
London
WC2A 3BH
Tel: 020 740 47744

Springboard UK Ltd
3 Denmark Street
London
WC2H 8LP
Tel: 020 7497 8654

Wine and Spirit Education
Trust
5 King's House
1 Queen Street Place
London
EC4R 1QS
Tel: 020 7246 1535

### Food Photographer
The Association of
Photographers
81 Leonard Street
London
EC2A 4QS
Tel: 020 7739 6669

British Institute of
Professional Photography
Fox Talbot House
2 Amwell End
Ware, Hertfordshire
SG12 9HN
Tel: 01920 464011

## Australia
National Training
Information Service
Australian National
Training Authority
Level 17, 200 Mary Street,
Brisbane QLD 4000
GPO Box 3120
Tel: (07) 3246 2300

5/321 Exhibition Street
Melbourne, VIC 3000
GPO Box 5347BB
Melbourne VIC 3001
Tel: (03) 9630 9800

Food Australia
PO Box 6436
Alexandria NSW 2015
Australia
Tel: 61 28399 3996

## New Zealand
kiwicareers.govt.nz
Tel: 0800 222733

New Zealand Institute of
Food Science and
Technology
PO Box 8031
Palmerston North
New Zealand
Tel: 64 6356 1686

## South Africa
South African Association
for Food Science and
Technology
c/o Kraft Foods
South Africa
PO Box 12029
Chloorkop. 1624

# Index